Michael
JORDAN

MICHAEL JORDAN
Basketball Superstar
& Commercial Icon

by Jeff Hawkins

ABDO
Publishing Company

Published by ABDO Publishing Company, PO Box 398166, Minneapolis, MN 55439. Copyright © 2014 by Abdo Consulting Group, Inc. International copyrights reserved in all countries. No part of this book may be reproduced in any form without written permission from the publisher. SportsZone™ is a trademark and logo of ABDO Publishing Company.

Printed in the United States of America,
North Mankato, Minnesota
102013
012014

Editor: Holly Saari
Series Designer: Christa Schneider

Library of Congress Control Number: 2013946587

Cataloging-in-Publication Data

Hawkins, Jeff.
 Michael Jordan: basketball superstar & commercial icon / Jeff Hawkins.
   p. cm. -- (Legendary athletes)
Includes bibliographical references and index.
ISBN 978-1-62403-130-4
1.   Jordan, Michael, 1963- --Juvenile literature.   2. Basketball players--United States--Biography--Juvenile literature.   1. Title.
796.323/092--dc23
[B]

                                                    2013946587

TABLE OF CONTENTS

CHAPTER 1

By the 1992 Olympics, Michael Jordan had several successful seasons playing professional basketball.

Dream Team Star

Michael Jordan was becoming upset. His team had started slowly and now trailed 16–7. He called for a time-out. It was only a practice, but to Jordan it was unacceptable for his team to merely go through the motions. Jordan and the other original Dream Team members were scrimmaging during a practice at the 1992 Olympic Games in Barcelona, Spain. They needed to work harder if they were to be ready for the next round.

Approximately 12 hours earlier, the US men's basketball team overwhelmed France 111–71 during an exhibition game. No one on Team USA, however, was satisfied with the performance. France held leads of 8–2 and 16–13 before the Dream Team awoke from its early slumber.

At the scrimmage, Jordan was daring his teammates, an unprecedented collection of All-Stars and future Hall of Famers, to step up their game. Jordan's team was pitted against that of Earvin "Magic" Johnson. Jordan relished the

Despite a personal rivalry, Jordan, *right*, and Magic Johnson had good chemistry on the court at the 1992 Olympics.

matchup. At the time, Jordan was still proving he deserved to be in the conversation about the world's best player. He saw the scrimmage as an opportunity to go against the recently retired Johnson. Throughout the 1980s and early 1990s, many National Basketball Association (NBA) insiders believed Johnson was the best, but that opinion was changing rapidly.

After the time-out, Jordan's team got to work. With more fluidity during the next offensive set, Jordan ran a play where he darted through the lane and cut to his left. He received a pass from center Patrick Ewing, an 11-time NBA All-Star, and hit a jump shot. Later, with his team leading 28–26, Jordan released an open jumper after future Hall of Famer Chris Mullin reacted slowly on defense. Just before the scrimmage's end, Jordan

Dream Team Rock Stars

Wherever and whenever the Dream Team ventured out to take in Olympic sites, the event was covered by a throng of journalists. There was so much media attention, the players and coaches could not sleep at the Olympic Village with the other athletes. "It was like traveling with 12 rock stars," said coach Chuck Daly, then-coach of the Bulls rival Detroit Pistons. "It was like Elvis and the Beatles put together."[1]

Immediately after blowouts, some foreign players appeared less concerned with the defeat than with finding time to pose for pictures with the US stars. A few opposing players actually attempted to pose *during* games.

again drove the lane and drew a foul from Christian Laettner, college basketball's player of the year for 1991–92. Jordan hit both free throws just prior to the end of what *Sports Illustrated* later described as "the Greatest Game Nobody Ever Saw."[2] Final score: Jordan's White Team 40, Johnson's Blue Team 36.

Jordan usually played in front of sold-out crowds, but the setting for this practice was different. There were few spectators, no sportswriters, and no league officials. To Jordan, it did not matter. Practice was just as serious as a game. His intensity is what helped him capture six NBA championships, two Olympic

Dream Team Roster Revealed

The first 10 members of the Dream Team were announced on September 21, 1991. Headlining the superstar lineup were guard-forward Jordan, forward Larry Bird of the Boston Celtics, and guard-forward Magic Johnson, formerly of the Los Angeles Lakers.

Seven more future Hall of Famers were also on the roster. The Utah Jazz connection of power forward Karl Malone and point guard John Stockton added a dependable inside-outside combination. Forward Charles Barkley of the Phoenix Suns packed up his bigger-than-life personality and teamed with centers Patrick Ewing of the New York Knicks and David Robinson of the San Antonio Spurs to form a formidable front court. Forward Scottie Pippen, Jordan's longtime teammate with the Chicago Bulls, and jump-shot artist Chris Mullin of the Golden State Warriors also were introduced during the initial announcement gathering. Portland Trail Blazers guard Clyde Drexler and former Duke University star Christian Laettner were selected to round out the roster.

gold medals, a Pan American Games gold medal, and a National Collegiate Athletic Association (NCAA) national championship during his career.

Dream Player on the Dream Team

More than two decades after their exploits, the original Dream Team is still widely recognized as the greatest basketball squad ever assembled. The 1992 Olympics was the first Summer Games at which professional players could perform, so Team USA was loaded with NBA superstars. Team USA's marketing targeted the "Big Three": Jordan, Johnson, and Larry Bird. The trio has long been credited with helping reshape the NBA's image in the 1980s, sparking unprecedented interest in the sport. But even in a locker room occupied by some of the best players of all time, Jordan stood out.

The previous spring, he guided the Chicago Bulls to their second consecutive NBA championship. He was also the reigning six-time scoring champion and league Most Valuable Player (MVP) in 1988 and 1991. A versatile scorer, Jordan was known for his trademark slam dunks. He also worked diligently to improve his jump shot. His athleticism allowed him to aggressively drive the lane and draw fouls. Later in his career, Jordan developed a post-up, fadeaway jump shot. It proved extremely difficult to defend.

From the start, Jordan was the dream player on the Dream Team. His talent, leadership, and work ethic helped ignite the squad's chemistry.

Dream Team Earns Gold

The Dream Team's talent simply overwhelmed the world. Team USA averaged 117.3 points per game and was the first team at the Olympics to score more than 100 points in each game. En route to capturing the gold medal, the squad routed its eight Olympic opponents by an average margin of 43.8 points.

To reach its gold-medal goal, Team USA faced one final speed bump: Croatia. Surrounded by a tremendous amount of pregame hoopla, the gold-medal game started with Jordan establishing a quick tempo. He scored four of his team's first eight points,

Jordan's First Olympic Gold

Jordan is one of only three US men's basketball players to claim Olympic gold medals as a professional and an amateur. As an amateur, Jordan teamed with future Dream Teamers Patrick Ewing and Chris Mullin to lead Team USA to an 8–0 record during the 1984 Summer Games in Los Angeles, California.

At the Games, Jordan averaged 17.1 points per game to lead the squad highlighted by several future NBA stars. In the gold-medal game, Jordan scored a team-high 20 points during a 96–65 victory over Spain.

with his teammates feeding off their leader's early energy.

Team USA had to regroup after Croatia scored 10 unanswered points, claiming a 25–23 lead with 9:35 to go until halftime. Jordan helped the players regroup by doing what he did best—lead by example. The Dream Team responded with a 15–2 spurt. The run was highlighted by Jordan, the NBA's best finisher, capping a Ewing-led fast break with an open-court slam dunk. From there, the Dream Team cruised to a 117–85 victory, earning the gold. During the international tournament, Jordan hit 51 of 113 field-goal attempts, averaging 14.9 points per game. He also added 4.8 assists and 2.4 rebounds per game.

Jordan helped solidify his reputation as the game's top athlete with his groundbreaking performance during the 1992

Dream Team's Legacy

The original Dream Team left a lasting legacy. In 2010, the entire squad was inducted into the Naismith Memorial Basketball Hall of Fame. As individuals, 11 of the 12 players and three of the four coaches had been previously inducted. The Dream Team's biggest impact likely came in the global recognition the NBA received. Since the Dream Team captured the world's attention in 1992, the quantity and quality of international NBA players has dramatically improved. Prior to the 1991–92 season, only 23 foreign players from 18 countries were on NBA rosters. By 2011–12, those numbers were up to 74 players from 35 countries.

Summer Games. After the Olympics, he would create some of the most famous moments in NBA history. Eventually winning six NBA titles with the Chicago Bulls, Jordan easily proved to be one of the greatest players in basketball history.

Jordan, *center*, stands with the Dream Team during the gold-medal ceremony at the 1992 Olympic Games in Barcelona, Spain.

CHAPTER 2

Michael Jordan grew up in Wilmington, North Carolina, and remained in the state for college basketball.

Growing Up

Michael Jeffrey Jordan was born on February 17, 1963, in Brooklyn, New York. He was the fourth child of five born to James Sr. and Deloris Jordan. Before Michael's first birthday, the Jordans moved to Wilmington, North Carolina, where Michael spent the rest of his childhood. From an early age, James Sr. and Deloris taught their children to approach hard work with a positive attitude.

Competitive and Athletic

Michael's ultracompetitive nature as an NBA superstar can be traced to his home environment. If he and his two older brothers, older sister, and younger sister were not playing basketball, playing catch, or throwing around a football, they usually were engaged in intense contests of checkers or other board games. James Sr. even constructed two wooden backboards with rims and placed them at opposite ends of the backyard. Before long, the grass was beaten down and the dirt was as hard and smooth as a court. During daily backyard games, Michael could not beat his brother Larry, but he kept trying.

Although Michael was smaller than most of the boys his age, he was a natural athlete. In 1975, 12-year-old Michael started to develop a reputation as one of the area's top youth baseball players. As a pitcher, shortstop, and outfielder, Michael was named Mr. Baseball as the MVP for the Dixie Youth Baseball Association. Upon entering Trask Middle School, Michael was known as one of the school's top athletes. In June 1977, Michael won certificates of achievement for baseball and football and was named the school's outstanding athlete.

Sophomore and Junior Years

In high school his athleticism continued. In 1978, as a sophomore at Emsley A. Laney High School, Michael started at quarterback on the junior varsity (JV) football team. After that season, Michael attempted to land a spot on the boys' varsity basketball team. Coach Clifton "Pop" Herring believed the 5-foot-9 athlete had talent. But he knew Michael would benefit more from a season at the JV level, where he could participate on the starting squad, than on the varsity team, where he would get less playing time.

Michael was devastated he did not make varsity and thought briefly about quitting the game. Instead, Jordan took his parents' teachings to heart and started working harder. On the JV squad, Michael dramatically improved his fundamentals and became the team's offensive catalyst, averaging nearly 28 points per game.

The summer going into his junior year, Michael practiced hard at his family's backyard court. In the fall, Michael made varsity and quickly emerged as the program's top point guard. A lot was expected from the first-year varsity starter. Through the opening month of the season, however, Michael struggled. He was trying too hard to force plays, and he soon lost confidence.

Michael felt his starting role was in jeopardy as the Laney Buccaneers entered a local holiday tournament. But in the tournament final against rival New Hanover

Michael Jordan, Team Manager

During Michael's sophomore year, Laney's varsity team enjoyed a winning season and needed to promote a player to round out the bench for the state tournament. Michael again tried out, but Herring brought up Michael's friend, 6-foot-8 Leroy Smith. Herring said the decision came down to the Buccaneers needing Smith's rebounding and size more than Michael's scoring and hustle.

Determined to go to the tournament with the varsity team, Michael learned the team manager was ill and could not make the trip. Michael volunteered to carry the equipment and sit at the end of the bench and pass out towels during the game. The experience made him even more determined to never sit on the bench again.

High, something clicked, and Michael easily took command of the court. Trailing by one point in the closing seconds, Michael pulled up for a jumper and swished it as the buzzer sounded. Michael, wearing his familiar No. 23 jersey, scored Laney's final 15 points to lead the team to victory.

Top College Recruit

During the second half of his junior year, Michael emerged as a top college recruit and received scholarship offers from a number of major Division I programs. Among his early favorites were Duke University, North Carolina State University, Syracuse University, and the University of North Carolina (UNC). Many close to Michael believed he would sign with the North Carolina State Wolfpack. During his youth, the Wolfpack were his favorite team, and former star David Thompson was his favorite player.

Michael first appeared on the UNC Tar Heels' radar when a school official watched him play late in his junior season. That summer, Michael attended

Jordan's Height

During the summer between his sophomore and junior basketball seasons, Michael grew six inches, from 5-foot-9 to 6-foot-3. Many of those close to Jordan often wondered how he eventually grew to nearly 6-foot-6, which he reached in college. Michael's father James Sr. and brother Larry were around 5-foot-6 and James Jr. was around 5-foot-7. "I think Michael just willed himself to grow," James Sr. said years later.[1]

UNC's summer camp and impressed coach Dean Smith and his staff. "When I first saw him, he jumped out at me because of his athleticism and competitiveness," UNC assistant coach Bill Guthridge said. "I thought we should recruit him, but I didn't know how good he would be."[2] Michael had an opportunity to get to know Smith during a recruiting visit to UNC. Afterward, Michael officially announced his commitment to join the Tar Heels.

Senior Year

Michael's confidence soared as a senior, and he dominated the competition. Michael averaged 29.2 points, 11.6 rebounds, and 10.1 assists per game,

Keeping North Carolina Players

The UNC men's basketball team had long developed a reputation as one of the country's top programs by traditionally recruiting top players from New York City. Coach Dean Smith adopted a new recruiting style. He concentrated more on in-state prospects.

The 1981 class showed the benefits. Not only did Smith land Michael Jordan, but he also signed Robert "Buzz" Peterson Jr. of Asheville, North Carolina. Most observers ranked Peterson as the best high school player in the state. Local product James Worthy was another key member of the Tar Heels during the early 1980s. "Coach Smith had a rule that we didn't want to ever bypass a player from North Carolina," former assistant coach Bill Guthridge said. "If there was a real good player in [North Carolina], we didn't want to lose him."[3] Without that rule, the Tar Heels might have let Michael get away.

Skipping Class to Practice

After scoring the game-winning points in the holiday tournament his junior year, Michael was determined to improve all aspects of his game. He started spending hours practicing at the Laney gymnasium. Michael practiced before school, after school, and sometimes during school. Early in his senior year, Michael cut biology class and went to the gymnasium to practice. He attempted the trick for about a week until he was caught. He received a suspension from school and a severe reprimand from his parents. To James Sr. and Deloris, academics were more important than athletics. Michael learned he needed to balance school and basketball.

becoming the first player in North Carolina history to average a triple-double. A triple-double is when a player has at least 10 in three different statistics. Foreshadowing his late-game heroics at the college and professional levels, with just 11 seconds remaining on the clock, Michael connected on a set of game-clinching free throws at the 1981 McDonald's All-American High School Basketball Game. With a then-record 30-point performance, Michael led the East squad to a 96–95 victory. It would not be long until he was leading at the collegiate level as well.

Dean Smith was Michael's coach throughout his time at UNC.

CHAPTER 3

During his freshman year, Michael Jordan proved to be a key player for UNC.

UNC

Early in his first semester at UNC, Jordan was having a tough time with the transition into college life. He felt overwhelmed and homesick. With the help of his roommate, freshman guard Buzz Peterson, Jordan started to feel more relaxed on and off the court.

When the Tar Heels' practice officially opened for the 1981–82 season, there was only one vacancy on the starting unit: shooting guard. Few expected Jordan to earn the spot as a freshman. Previously, only three other first-year players had started for Dean Smith. A few weeks into practice, however, the coaching staff noticed no one on the team could guard Jordan one-on-one. On the day of the much-anticipated opener against the University of Kansas Jayhawks, Jordan saw his name on the starting lineup for a matchup that would be televised all along the East Coast. Jordan was a bit nervous, but he quickly fell into his stride early in the game, maneuvering past two defenders and connecting on a short jumper.

Jordan's confidence grew with each game and each practice. During his third game, UNC earned a 78–70 win over a tough University of Tulsa squad at home in Chapel Hill. Jordan displayed his versatility by scoring 22 points on 11-of-15 shooting, grabbing 5 rebounds, dishing out 3 assists, and creating 4 steals. He did all that in just 22 minutes of action.

NCAA Champs

Sparked by Jordan's emergence, the Tar Heels finished the regular season 24–2 and captured the regular-season and tournament championships in the Atlantic Coast Conference (ACC). They entered the NCAA Tournament ranked number one and qualified for the championship game against the Patrick Ewing–led Georgetown University Hoyas on March 29, 1982. The matchup was close, and the Tar Heels trailed by one point with just 32 seconds remaining. But with 15 seconds remaining, Jordan caught a pass and nailed a 16-foot jumper, pulling the Tar Heels ahead 63–62. Jordan's last basket of

Jordan's Work Ethic

Coach Dean Smith won 879 games and two national titles during his 36 years at UNC. Years later, Jordan's work ethic still impressed Smith. "One thing about Michael that stood out was how hard he worked," Smith said. "We expected he'd get better because of that, and he did, year after year. A player with that kind of talent who works as hard as Michael did has a chance to do great things, and he was smart about it. He'd listen closely to what the coaches said and then go do it."[1]

Jordan shoots the winning basket during the 1982 NCAA championship game.

the game clinched the championship for UNC. Jordan was named the ACC Freshman of the Year, averaging 13.5 points per game.

But the championship celebration did not last long for Jordan. Even after all he accomplished, he was determined to improve. Two days after winning the title, Jordan was back at the gym, working on fundamentals, particularly his sometimes-lacking defensive game.

Sophomore Season

During the summer, Jordan spent hours and hours at the gymnasium improving his defensive skills. His improvements paid dividends from the start of practice for the 1982–83 season. "We couldn't believe how good he was as a sophomore," Guthridge said. "We ran a drill in practice where players went one-on-one against each other. There was nobody who could stop Michael and Michael could stop everyone. That was really something then."[2]

Led by Jordan, the Tar Heels finished the season 28–8, falling to the University of Georgia in the regional finals of the NCAA tournament. Jordan

Jordan Comes through on Defense

Jordan proved as a freshman he could develop into a prolific scorer. On defense, however, he struggled at times. But when it counted most, as during the 1982 NCAA tournament, Jordan came through. Moments after his 16-foot jump shot gave UNC the 63–62 lead over Georgetown with 15 seconds remaining, Jordan hustled back on defense. Because of this, he was able to play a role in the Hoyas' turnover that sealed the championship. "Georgetown turned it over because Michael got back on defense and made a play in the passing lane," UNC coach Dean Smith explained.[3]

Jordan made it a habit to continuously work on his defense. As a sophomore, Jordan was named team defensive player of the game 12 times. By his junior season, Smith allowed Jordan to freelance from the defense's disciplined structure to go for a steal. Up to that point, Jordan was only the third player Smith granted this freedom.

averaged 20.0 points per game and earned first-team All-America honors. But the early tourney exit stung Jordan, who did not wait long to begin his off-season conditioning program.

Junior Season

His hard work was not noticeable in the beginning of the 1983–84 campaign, as Jordan suffered through his first extended shooting slump. Jordan had not played so poorly since the start of his junior season in high school. He sought help from his father, who advised him to stop forcing plays, relax, and take the game to his opponents.

The advice worked. Jordan's performance against the Louisiana State University Tigers on January 29, 1984, proved the turning point of his season. He scored 29 points and

1983 Pan American Games

As a college star, Jordan was chosen to play on Team USA for the 1983 Pan American Games in Caracas, Venezuela. The Pan American Games are an Olympic-style, multisport event involving athletes from North America, Central America, and South America. After a sluggish first half against Brazil, Team USA needed a lift, and Jordan provided it. He glided down the baseline, jumped, and executed a two-handed dunk. Over the next several minutes, Jordan took control, hitting five of six shots as Team USA rallied to top Brazil 87–79. The Americans went on to win the gold medal, going 8–0 during the tournament. The trip had another benefit too. Inspired by the culture in Venezuela, Jordan changed his emphasis of studies at UNC to cultural geography. If a professional basketball career did not work out, Jordan wanted to be a geography teacher.

led the Tar Heels to a 90–79 rout. From that outing, Jordan led the Tar Heels to the ACC regular-season title. The Tar Heels entered the NCAA Tournament as a top seed, but the team was ousted by the underdog Indiana University Hoosiers in the Sweet Sixteen.

Weeks later, Jordan was still upset. Amid his lingering tournament frustrations of the past two seasons, Jordan took solace in being named college basketball's player of the year. He also was named first-team All-America for the second year in a row.

Moving On

Outside speculation was heating up regarding Jordan's immediate future. Would he return for a senior season or move on to the professional level? To help in the decision, Smith invited the Jordans and their son to his office for a meeting. Smith was confident Jordan's game would thrive in the NBA. Jordan's mother wanted her son to return for a senior season. Jordan's father wanted him to declare for the upcoming NBA Draft. No longer the wiry, homesick teenager that he was when he first arrived in Chapel Hill, Jordan decided it was time to move to the next level.

Jordan blocks a shot during a January 1984 game.

CHAPTER 4

Chicago Bulls rookie Michael Jordan slam dunks the ball during a game against the Milwaukee Bucks during the 1984–85 season.

Playing in the Pros

As the Chicago Bulls collected scouting reports on potential choices for the 1984 draft, one player stuck out to general manager Rod Thorn: Michael Jordan, a junior out of UNC. The Bulls did not schedule Jordan to come to Chicago Stadium for a pre-draft workout. But Thorn made several trips to visit Dean Smith at UNC, where he got a glowing report of Jordan's college play and potential in the NBA.

To prepare for the NBA Draft, Jordan spent his time running and playing golf in the mornings. In the afternoons, he spent time in the gym playing pickup basketball with friends and former teammates. In the evenings, he studied his correspondence courses to fulfill the promise to his mother about earning his college degree. By the day of the draft, the Bulls had made their decision. They used their number three pick to choose Jordan, setting in motion a franchise-changing experience.

Trendsetter

During his rookie season, Jordan made a couple early fashion statements. He wore black sneakers with bold red stripes. His style of wearing an armband halfway up his left arm would soon be adopted by legions of young players across the nation. When asked why he started doing that, he responded by rubbing the back of his arm across his forehead. "I have it there because I do [that] all the time," he said. "I can't wear it on my wrist because the sweat would get on my hand."[3]

Rookie Season

During NBA training camp, Bulls coach Kevin Loughery started developing an offensive game plan centered on Jordan, but the rookie did not start the Bulls' preseason opener against the Indiana Pacers. When he entered the game later, Jordan played point guard. He finished with 18 points and eight rebounds. "I was nervous," he told sportswriters after the game. "But I'm OK after I run up and down the court a few times. That gets it out of my system."[1]

During his second exhibition appearance against the host Kansas City Kings, Jordan scored 32 points. He was 10 of 11 from the field and 12 of 13 from the free-throw line. "And if you think he was good in the game, you should have seen him in practice," Bulls scout Mike Thibault said.[2]

In his first regular-season game, Jordan collected 16 points, 6 rebounds, and 7 assists. After his third game, Thorn realized Jordan was just beginning to realize his potential. Jordan went face-to-face with Milwaukee Bucks guard Sidney Moncrief. The two-time

NBA Defensive Player of the Year could not contain the rookie. Moncrief needed help. Double-teams did not seem to matter. "In the fourth quarter, I don't care if they double or triple-teamed him or whatever they did, he still scored," Thorn recalled. "We ended up beating them and it was like, 'Goodness gracious, I can't believe what I just saw out there.'"[4]

About a month into his NBA career, *Sports Illustrated* released a cover featuring Jordan. The headline read, "A Star Is Born."[5] It did not take long for NBA fans to embrace Jordan's all-out playing style. Even at opposing arenas, Jordan often received ovations during pregame introductions. The fans

Jordan's All-Star Freeze-Out

Rookie Jordan had a curious stat line for the 1985 NBA All-Star Game. Jordan had just seven points. The curiosity ended when word soon leaked that Detroit Pistons guard Isiah Thomas, Jordan's All-Star teammate, conducted a Jordan "freeze-out." Most of the East All-Stars did not pass to Jordan. He still made his cuts and worked to get open. He just rarely received the ball in position to score. Thomas apparently was jealous of Jordan's rising popularity. As Central Division rivals, Thomas attempted to put Jordan in his place.

The Pistons were a team Jordan felt a strong rivalry with, especially in the late 1980s and early 1990s. That is when the Pistons captured consecutive NBA championships. To become a champion himself, Jordan first had to topple the Pistons. Never forgetting Thomas's snub in the 1985 game, Jordan reportedly made sure Thomas was not part of the 1992 Olympic Dream Team.

Air Jordans

In 1985, Nike released the Air Jordan I sneaker to much fanfare. The first color arrangement came in red and black, matching the Chicago Bulls' color scheme. The brand was an immediate hit among teenaged consumers. When Jordan first started wearing the shoes in the NBA, he was fined $5,000 per game because NBA policy stated shoes had to match those worn by teammates, and the Air Jordans did not. New editions of the shoes were released annually. As of 2013, nearly 30 years after they were introduced and a decade after Jordan's retirement as a player, Jordan-brand shoes took nearly 60 percent of the basketball shoe market.

spoke on his rising popularity, voting him a starter for the NBA All-Star Game. Just two days after, on February 12, 1985, Jordan set a Bulls' single-game rookie scoring record, unleashing 49 points against the Detroit Pistons.

Assuming the role of franchise savior, Jordan helped lead the Bulls to an improved 38–44 record, which qualified them for the playoffs. But they lost to the Milwaukee Bucks in the first round. After averaging 28.2 points per game, good for third in the league, Jordan was named NBA Rookie of the Year. He was just getting started.

Second Season

If prodded, Jordan would sometimes show off his unique jumping ability. He was able to leap and get his entire hand over the square on the backboard. Some people just could not believe it until they saw it. Throughout his career, Jordan played with reckless abandon. He aggressively drove the lane, seeking body contact. He dived for loose balls. He crashed the boards. He absorbed charging calls on defense.

Despite his all-out style, Jordan remained relatively healthy throughout his career. He only endured one extended stay on the sidelines due to injury. That occurred in the third game of the 1985–86 season. Jordan broke a bone in his foot and missed 64 games. Returning in mid-March, Jordan averaged career lows in scoring (22.7), rebounds (3.6), and assists (2.9).

But by the playoffs, Jordan had his game back. He made a statement against the Bulls' first-round opponent, the Boston Celtics, considered by many NBA insiders to be one of the top teams of all time. In Game 2, Jordan put on an unforgettable display of scoring. But his NBA playoff-record 63 points were not enough. The Celtics earned a 135–131 victory in double overtime. "Michael was doing so much and so well, I found myself just wanting to stop and watch him—and I was playing,"[6] teammate John Paxson said. Although the Celtics won the round in a three-game sweep, Jordan averaged 43.7 points per game. Celtics legend Larry Bird marveled at his younger opponent. "I didn't think anyone was capable of doing what Michael has done to us," Bird said. "He is the most exciting, awesome player in the game today. I think it's just God disguised as Michael Jordan."[7]

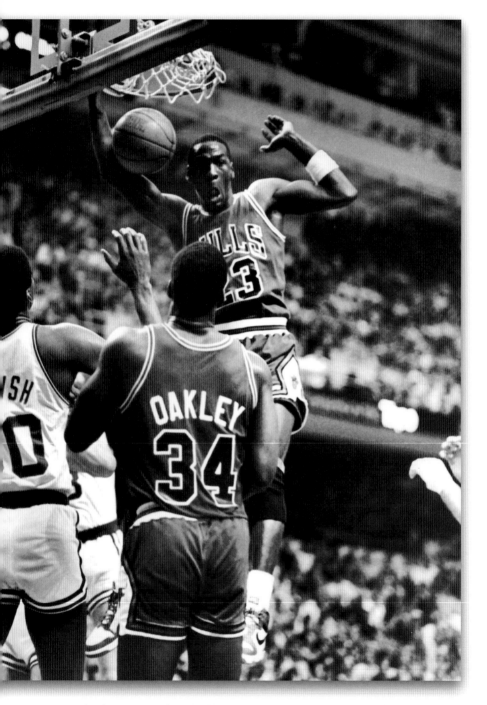

Jordan reacts after dunking the ball against the Boston Celtics in an April 1986 playoff game.

Golden Era

The 1980s were a golden era for the NBA. The on-court rivalry of Boston's Bird and Magic Johnson of the Los Angeles Lakers sparked interest in casual fans. The up-tempo, high-scoring spectacles created excitement in the sporting world.

Jordan was a perfect fit for the league's up-and-coming fast-breaking style. Completely recovered from the previous season's injury, Jordan enjoyed one of the top scoring seasons of all time in 1986–87. He finished with 3,041 points. As of 2013, only Jordan and Hall of Famer Wilt Chamberlain had eclipsed the 3,000-point milestone in a single season. Averaging 37.1 points per game, Jordan claimed the first of seven consecutive individual scoring titles.

Jordan set a tone for the season early on. During a streak in late November and early December, Jordan scored 40 or more points in nine consecutive starts. Later in the season, Jordan put on a dizzying scoring display against the Atlanta Hawks. On his way to

Slam Dunk Champion

In his rookie season, Jordan placed second in the NBA Slam Dunk Contest. After sitting out the next year with an injury, Jordan claimed his first midseason showcase title in 1987. Jordan's best effort came on his trademark leap from the free-throw line. It was a repeat dunk from 1985, but this version was more fluid, and fans could clearly see his tongue dangling out of his mouth, another trademark of his. Another dunk, which saw Jordan leap sideways and hang in the air briefly before leaning toward the rim, also brought loud applause.

recording 61 points, Jordan scored 23 points in a row, an NBA record.

Jordan was establishing himself as the league's prime scoring threat, but he continued to work on his defense. He started showing flashes of stout defensive ability, becoming the first player to collect 200 steals and 100 blocks during the 1986–87 season.

Despite Jordan's all-around performance, the Bulls finished the regular season at 40–42. For the second year in a row, the Bulls drew the Celtics in the opening round of the playoffs. For the second year in a row, the Bulls were swept. The front office was frustrated over the Bulls' early playoff exits in Jordan's first three seasons, but success for the team was on the horizon.

CHAPTER 5

Michael Jordan soars in the air during the 1988 Slam Dunk Contest.

Jordan had one of the highest verticals in the NBA.

Chasing the Championship

By the 1987–88 season, Jordan had become a celebrity. It seemed he could be seen or heard everywhere. He was on television commercials, magazine covers, late-night talk shows, and radio.

As popular as he was, Jordan still had not found success in the playoffs, and it was gnawing at him. He needed to be surrounded by better talent. Help arrived in the form of rookies Scottie Pippen and Horace Grant, and Jordan saw the Chicago Bulls lineup improving during training camp.

Taking the Next Step

Utilizing the rookie duo's talents, Jordan became more of a playmaker. Understanding the Bulls needed him to be more than just a scorer, Jordan set more picks and passed the ball more to his supporting cast. He still led the Bulls in scoring in 81 of 82 regular-season games, but insiders credited him for becoming a more complete player.

One-of-a-Kind Season

By the 1987–88 season, Jordan was quickly developing into the world's best all-around basketball player. Jordan became the first player in NBA history to be named the league's MVP and Defensive Player of the Year in the same year. Plus, he established a record for blocks by a guard. Jordan also helped dispel the notion he tended to be selfish with the basketball. While leading the league in scoring, he also averaged 5.9 assists per game.

His popularity soared even higher. As the regular season came to an end, Jordan had scored a league-high 35.0 points per game, helping the Bulls finish 50–32. Jordan earned his first NBA regular-season MVP Award. He claimed several other major awards as well: Defensive Player of the Year, All-Star Game MVP, and the individual scoring title. He even placed first in the NBA Slam Dunk Contest.

In the first round of the playoffs against the Cleveland Cavaliers, Jordan played like the league's best player. In Game 1, when his young teammates appeared overwhelmed by postseason pressure, Jordan scored nearly half of the Bulls' points in a 104–93 victory. In Game 2, Jordan scored 55 points in a 106–101 victory. But despite Jordan averaging 41.0 points during Games 3 and 4, the Bulls lost. It was as if the young Bulls players stepped back to allow Jordan to win the five-game series by himself. Jordan scored 39 in the deciding fifth game, leading the Bulls to a 107–101 victory.

The Bulls played the Detroit Pistons in the second round. The Pistons studied how Jordan almost single-handedly beat the Cavaliers in the first round. Pistons coach Chuck Daly devised a game plan to stop the dazzling star. If they could neutralize Jordan, no one else would be able to step up, Daly figured.

The special defense was called the "Jordan rules." Whenever Jordan received the ball, All-Star guard Joe Dumars defended him aggressively. Before Jordan could make a move, a second defender appeared to cut off his drive to the basket. If Jordan escaped the double-team, bruising forwards Bill Laimbeer, Rick Mahorn, or Dennis Rodman would execute a hard foul.

Jordan Claims Second Slam Dunk Title

On his opening effort at the 1988 NBA Slam Dunk Contest, Jordan jumped to the basket while putting the ball between his legs and then over his head. He finished it off with a two-handed reverse slam. To reach the finals, he took off from the baseline, leaned sideways, and reached around the rim for a windmill slam dunk.

In the finals, Jordan executed his trademark jump from the free-throw line. This time, he double-clutched in midair before slamming the ball through the hoop. The judges gave Jordan a perfect 50 for his final dunk, which assured him the victory.

But the Slam Dunk Contest had its controversy. The judges at Chicago Stadium awarded a score of 45 to Atlanta Hawks star Dominique Wilkins after a difficult third dunk. Many believed the dunk deserved more and wondered if the judges gave a lower score on purpose. Jordan captured his second Slam Dunk Contest by two points.

One of Jordan's trademarks was his tongue hanging out as he played.

Often, Jordan was knocked down. But he just got back up. Still Daly's defense worked, and none of the Bulls' rising youngsters stepped up. The Bulls dropped the series in five games. The Bulls-Pistons playoff series was a preview for a growing rivalry.

More Pistons Problems

In his fifth NBA season, Jordan was on fire and could not be stopped. He was so dominating that triple-teams were often pointless. When the regular season ended, Jordan averaged 32.5 points per game and led the league in scoring—again. He established career highs in rebounds (8.0) and assists (8.0) per game. Jordan also ranked third in the NBA with 2.9 steals per outing. On January 25, 1989, Jordan recorded his 10,000th career point.

The Bulls finished the regular season 47–35, setting up a memorable five-game playoff series against the Cavaliers. The first-round series was capped by what has become known as "the Shot." The Bulls trailed by one point when Jordan was passed the ball. With two seconds left in the game, Jordan rose over Cavaliers guard Craig Ehlo to shoot a buzzer-beating basket. The play is embedded in NBA lore. Jordan's clutch effort clinched the 101–100 victory and moved the Bulls to the second round. After cruising through the second round, the Bulls once again faced the Pistons. And once again they were neutralized by the "Jordan rules."

Although he had not led the Bulls to a championship yet, the Bulls made sure Jordan would not enter the free-agent market for the next eight years. Management signed the star to a new contract. The $25 million deal, in 1989, was the biggest contract in NBA history. Still, the Bulls were itching to get to the next level, and to do that, they felt they needed a new coach. After the 1988–89 season, the Bulls hired coach Phil Jackson to give the franchise the boost it needed to get to the NBA Finals.

1989–90 Season

With Jackson in place as coach and Jordan firmly entrenched as franchise centerpiece, the Bulls, now with a core of seasoned veterans, arrived as a legitimate threat to claim a title in the 1989–90 season. Coached by Jackson and driven by Jordan's league-high 33.6 scoring average, the Bulls recorded a 55–27 record. It was the Bulls' best regular-season finish since 1971–72.

Jordan's regular season was highlighted by his career-high 69-point performance against the Cavaliers and his career-best 92 three-pointers. In his previous five seasons combined, Jordan had connected on only 58 three-pointers.

In the playoffs, the Bulls upended the Milwaukee Bucks in the first round and the Philadelphia 76ers in the second. For the second year in a row, the Pistons were waiting in the conference finals. And for the third year in a row, an element of the "Jordan rules" was in effect. The Bulls were eliminated in Game 7.

Angry over the lost opportunity to advance to the NBA Finals, Jordan retreated to the team bus after Game 7. "And I remember my father coming on the bus," Jordan said. "And I'm in the back, yelling and screaming at him. And he's doing his best to calm me down and say, 'It's only a game. You'll be given another opportunity.'"[1]

Jordan's dad was right. His time was coming.

Jordan's hang time allowed him to glide past taller players near the basket.

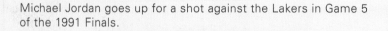

CHAPTER 6

Michael Jordan goes up for a shot against the Lakers in Game 5 of the 1991 Finals.

Three Championships

The 1990–91 regular season saw Jordan and the Chicago Bulls performing at full throttle. They finished with a 61–21 record and captured the Central Division title. It was the Bulls' first regular-season title since 1975. Jordan received his second league MVP Award after averaging 31.5 points per game. He was driven to make the NBA Finals.

As the Bulls entered the playoffs, Jordan said, "We're good enough to win it. We know we can beat the teams we're going to meet in the playoffs. My job is to take on the leadership role and take us to the next level."[1]

The Bulls backed up their leader's bravado by sweeping the New York Knicks in the first round and silencing the Philadelphia 76ers in five games in the next. Next up were the two-time defending league champions, the Detroit Pistons.

The Bulls took a different approach to counter the Pistons' "Jordan rules" tactic. Jordan intentionally played a secondary scoring role, and this time his teammates came through. The Bulls defeated the Pistons in a four-game sweep, qualifying for the NBA Finals for the first time in team history.

The Finals showdown was against the Los Angeles Lakers, and Jordan was eager to face one of the league's all-time best, Magic Johnson. The Lakers took charge of Game 1, slowing the pace of the game and methodically subduing the Bulls. In his first Finals appearance, Jordan had a chance to send the game into overtime, but his last-second jumper rolled around and out of the rim. The Bulls lost 93–91.

The Lakers seized the early momentum and carried it into Game 2. The Bulls needed a spark. Jordan accepted the challenge, delivering one of the most viewed drives of his career. After receiving the ball at the top of the key, Jordan

The Jordan Family

Jordan married Juanita Vanoy in 1989. The couple had two sons, Jeffrey and Marcus, and a daughter, Jasmine. Jeffrey and Marcus went on to play college basketball together at the University of Central Florida. In 2006, Michael and Juanita split up. The next year Juanita received a $168 million settlement for the divorce.

darted into the lane. As he leapt in the air, 6-foot-9 defender Sam Perkins stepped into position to detour Jordan's flight path. Jordan instantly leaned midair and switched the ball from his right to left hand while twisting away from his old UNC teammate. Jordan's improbable basket rallied the Bulls, leading them to a 107–86 victory.

In the deciding fifth game, Jordan played decoy. As soon as he touched the ball and was rushed, Jordan passed to an open teammate. The game plan worked, earning the Bulls a 108–101 victory and the Finals championship. As soon as the buzzer sounded, Jordan raced around, celebrating. "I never thought I'd be this emotional," Jordan later told a sportscaster. He continued:

> It was a seven-year struggle. When I first got to Chicago, we started from the bottom and every year we worked harder and harder 'til we got to it. I've appreciated so much in my life from my family, from my kids, everything, but this is my most proud day I've ever had.[2]

Jordan was named Finals MVP for the first time, with an average of 31.2 points and 11.4 assists per game.

Ready to Repeat

Jordan and the Bulls played off their momentum for the 1991–92 season. The team won a franchise-

Jordan shoots over Portland Trail Blazers guard Clyde Drexler during the 1992 Finals.

record 67 regular-season games, and Jordan was named league MVP. The Bulls reached the Finals again, where they were pitted against the Portland Trail Blazers.

Prior to Game 1, the media conjured up a Magic-Bird type rivalry by comparing Michael "Air" Jordan to Clyde "The Glide" Drexler. Known as two of the top combination guards of any era, Jordan and Drexler were athletic and played above the rim. The comparisons did not last long. In the first half of Game 1, Jordan scored 35 points, a Finals record. He had six three-pointers. After the sixth shot, Jordan jogged down the court and shrugged as he passed the television broadcasters.

Drexler was quoted throughout his career as saying his game was on par with Jordan's, but Jordan continuously outplayed Drexler in one-on-one matchups. Jordan's key basket over Drexler in Game 6 helped clinch the Bulls' second championship in two years. Jordan averaged 35.8 points per game during the Finals, securing his second series MVP honor. After winning his second NBA championship, Jordan put on another uniform to embark on the surreal summer experience of the original Dream Team.

The First Three-Peat

During the regular 1992–93 season, Jordan recorded his 20,000th career point. He blitzed the

Orlando Magic for 64 points, the Washington Bullets for 57, and the Lakers for 54. Jordan seized his seventh consecutive scoring title, tying Wilt Chamberlain's all-time record. He was named All-NBA First Team for the seventh time and All-Defensive First Team for the sixth.

For a third straight season, Jordan led the Bulls through the playoffs and to the Finals, where they met the Phoenix Suns. Jordan scorched them, scoring 40 or more points in four straight starts. Toppling the Suns in six games, the Bulls completed their "three-peat" with a third championship. Jordan averaged

Testing Toni Kukoc

During the 1992 off-season, Bulls management actively pursued and signed free agent Toni Kukoc of Croatia to a bigger contract than teammate Scottie Pippen. Jordan obviously felt his longtime teammate was slighted in contract negotiations.

After hearing so much about Kukoc's talent, Jordan wanted to give his new teammate a test when they met at the 1992 Olympic Games. Both members of the Dream Team, Jordan and Pippen decided to take turns guarding Kukoc during the first

meeting between Team USA and Croatia. It was called "the Kukoc Game." Jordan and Pippen played tenacious, in-your-face defense. "Dude, it was scary what they did to Kukoc," Dream Team teammate Charles Barkley said. "And beautiful to watch."[3] Center Patrick Ewing added, "They dogged Kukoc so bad. That was the best defense I ever saw Michael and Scottie play. By far. And they played a lot of great defense."[4] Obviously rattled, Kukoc was limited to 2-for-11 shooting during the 103–70 loss.

41.0 points per game to secure his third Finals MVP honor in a row. He was the first to accomplish the feat.

A Tragedy and Retirement

As Jordan settled into his 1993 off-season training schedule, his family was struck by an act of violence. Jordan's father, James Jordan Sr., was murdered on July 23, 1993. He apparently was asleep in his car at a highway rest area near Lumberton, North Carolina. Two teenagers were soon apprehended by authorities and sentenced to life in prison.

On October 6, a grieving Jordan held a press conference that stunned the collection of sportswriters and his fans—he announced he was retiring. Jordan said since he lost his father, he lost the desire to compete at the high level he

Jordan and Barkley

Jordan and Charles Barkley of the Phoenix Suns forged a close bond in 1992 during the Dream Team's gold-medal stroll. During their Olympic blowout wins, Barkley's competiveness never waned. He led Team USA in scoring with 18 points per game. The following spring, the friends met in the NBA Finals. Barkley's dominant play carried over into the 1993 play-offs. He averaged 26.6 points and 13.6 rebounds during the postseason, but Jordan would not be outshone. Jordan stole the Finals spotlight, scoring 31, 42, 44, 55, 41, and 33 points, respectively, in the six-game series. It was the Jordan-led Bulls' third consecutive championship.

Gambling

The pressure of Jordan's own celebrity was beginning to take its toll. During the Bulls' 1993 playoff run, witnesses saw Jordan gambling in a casino in Atlantic City, New Jersey, the night before a game against the New York Knicks. There were also reports that Jordan lost hundreds of thousands of dollars playing golf. In 2005, *60 Minutes* news anchor Ed Bradley interviewed Jordan on his past gambling addictions. "Yeah, I've gotten myself into situations where I would not walk away and I've pushed the envelope," Jordan said.[6]

demanded of himself. At the time, Jordan's 32.3 career scoring average was the highest in NBA history. The added exhaustion of winning three consecutive NBA championships and winning an Olympic gold medal with the Dream Team ultimately proved too much. "I have nothing more to prove in basketball," he said at the press conference.

"I have no more challenges. The death of my father made me realize how short life is."[5]

After the death of his father in 1993, Jordan announced his retirement from basketball.

Michael Jordan surprised fans when he signed a minor-league contract with the Chicago White Sox in February 1994.

From Basketball to Baseball and Back

If fans were surprised by Jordan's early retirement, they surely were flattened when they heard of Jordan's next athletic ambition. In February 1994, Jordan signed a minor-league contract with Major League Baseball's Chicago White Sox. Some in the media accused Jordan of pulling a publicity stunt. Few thought he would succeed. Jordan said he decided to play baseball in memory of his father. James Sr. always dreamed of seeing his youngest son play in the major leagues. "All I want is a chance to fulfill a dream," he said. "If I don't have the skills, I'll walk away from baseball."[1]

Jordan envisioned going straight to the White Sox. But after just a few days at spring training, it was evident he needed to start in the minor leagues. In three early exhibition games with the White Sox, Jordan looked awkward. He collected just three hits in his first 20 at bats. Jordan was assigned to minor-league camp.

New Career Challenges

As spring training ended, Jordan was assigned to the Birmingham Barons, the White Sox's AA affiliate based in Birmingham, Alabama. At 31 years old, Jordan was the oldest member of the Barons. At first, Jordan's new teammates were awestruck. Jordan did his best to fit in by not complaining much about the long bus rides and fast-food breaks. He was prepared to pay his dues.

Appearing in his first game with the Barons on April 8, 1994, Jordan went 0-for-3 and waited two more days before he recorded his first professional base hit. That sparked a 13-game hitting streak during which Jordan hit .378. Some scouts started to watch Jordan more closely. The hot streak soon ended, though, and his batting average hovered around .200 for much of the season. On July 30, Jordan connected on his first professional home run. It sparked a mini-renaissance in his swing and confidence. During August, Jordan hit .260 and proved to be a solid hitter with runners in scoring position. Despite a low batting average and a tendency to strike

Jordan the Actor

During Super Bowl XXVII in 1993, Jordan starred in a popular Nike commercial that blended live action with animation. In it, Jordan was paired with Looney Tunes character Bugs Bunny in a game of basketball against a team of Martians. The popularity of the advertisement inspired a full-length motion picture, *Space Jam*. Filmed during his retirement from the NBA, the movie was released in 1996 and went on to gross more than $230 million worldwide.

out, Jordan compiled 51 runs batted in. He still had hopes of making a run at the White Sox's roster the following spring.

But during the summer of 1994, the players walked away from contract negotiations and went on strike. The sides argued all winter. Major league teams decided to use replacement players to start the 1995 season if a new labor deal could not be reached. Jordan was asked if he wanted to be a replacement player and start the regular season in the majors. He declined. If he was going to make it to the major leagues, it would be by merit, he said.

Jordan's Summer in the Minors

With the Birmingham Barons, Jordan played right field and led all Southern League outfielders with 11 errors. At bat, Jordan hit just .202 with three home runs. In 436 at bats, he struck out 114 times. Jordan's speed was put to use, though, stealing 30 bases.

Back to the Bulls

As Jordan concentrated on improving his baseball swing, the Chicago Bulls struck out in their attempt to capture a fourth consecutive NBA championship in 1994. The quest ended in the playoffs' second round against the Patrick Ewing–led New York Knicks. In 1994–95, the Bulls were 34–31 entering the final stretch of the regular season. They needed a lift.

They got "Air." On March 18, 1995, Jordan again surprised sports fans around the world, when he

Jordan returned to the Bulls wearing No. 45, which was his number with the Birmingham Barons.

announced his return to the Bulls. The next day against the Indiana Pacers, he wore No. 45, which was his number as a minor-league baseball player. Creating a steal during his debut, Jordan streaked from one end of the court to the other to finish with a finger roll.

It appeared for a moment like classic Jordan. But for most of the outing, Jordan looked a step slow. He hit just 7 of 28 shots in a 103–96 loss to the host Pacers.

Jordan quickly rediscovered his shooting form. At the end of his fourth start, Jordan connected on a game-winning shot against the Atlanta Hawks. Ten days after announcing his comeback, Jordan went to Madison Square Garden and scored 55 points against the New York Knicks. Down the stretch, Jordan led the Bulls to a 13–4 record, helping the squad qualify for the playoffs. He led the team in scoring in 11 games, averaging 26.9 points per game.

But against the Orlando Magic in the Eastern Conference semifinals, the Bulls' streak ended. Near

Tough Workout Schedule

The Orlando Magic playoff failure made Jordan more determined than ever to return to past glory. To do so, Jordan needed to improve his physical condition. So he reenlisted the services of personal fitness trainer Tim Grover.

The off-season work began the day after the season ended. In seven years working with Grover, it was the earliest Jordan had ever started his workouts. Another difference Grover noticed was, for the first time, golf was not a top priority in Jordan's off-season. No longer were workouts scheduled around golf matches. Jordan's workout schedule began early in the morning with about 40 minutes of conditioning. Around lunchtime, Jordan lifted weights for about an hour. And he played pickup basketball in the evenings. By the start of training camp, Jordan was near the best shape of his career.

Jordan's Agent

Forward Scottie Pippen proved to be an invaluable on-court sidekick for Jordan's championship quests. With Pippen, Jordan found dependable support on the offensive and defensive ends of the court. Off the court, Jordan relied on another "teammate": David Falk. Jordan's agent handled the growing empire of endorsement deals. Falk developed the initial concept of the Air Jordan brand. "He's the best at what he does," Jordan said. "Marketing-wise, he's great."[2] Jordan trusted Falk to manage his responsibilities away from the court. That way, Jordan could focus and not have to worry too much about business.

the end of a close Game 1, Magic guard Nick Anderson guarded Jordan. In years past, Jordan would have commanded the moment. This time Anderson stripped the ball from Jordan, creating a turnover that led to a game-winning shot. After the game, Anderson proclaimed the new Jordan did not explode like the old one had. Jordan returned for Game 2 wearing his old No. 23 jersey and scored 38 points. Then he added 40 points in Game 3 and 39 more in Game 5. But it was not enough. The Bulls were eliminated in six games.

The summer turned into a time for the Bulls, as a franchise, to regroup and refocus. They would have Jordan for the entire next season. Jordan appeared hungry to prove he still could lead the Bulls to another championship.

Jordan drops in a layup against the Orlando Magic during the 1995 playoffs.

CHAPTER 8

Michael Jordan dribbles around a Seattle SuperSonics defender during the 1996 Finals.

Three More Rings

The competitive motivation that was missing for Jordan when he retired in 1993 had returned for the start of the 1995–96 season. With Jordan leading the charge, the new Chicago Bulls lineup meshed easily from the start of training camp.

Rarely had the Bulls ever played better—even during the previous three championship seasons. With a starting unit bolstered by the off-season acquisition of enigmatic former Detroit Piston Dennis Rodman, the Bulls finished the regular season 72–10, the NBA's best-ever regular-season record. Jordan averaged 30.4 points per game and claimed his NBA-record eighth scoring title. Jordan also joined Hall of Famer Willis Reed as the only players to be named league MVP, Finals MVP, and All-Star Game MVP during the same season.

The postseason accolades piled up for Jordan as they had before his retirement. But there was a difference in Jordan's play. He did not drive to the basket as often. He seemed to have lost some explosiveness off his first step. But he made up for the declining skills by refining his outside shooting, including his famous fadeaway shot.

The Bulls continued to cruise through the playoffs. With Jordan in command, the Bulls dropped just one game during the opening three rounds. In the NBA Finals against the Seattle SuperSonics, the Bulls streaked out to a 3–0 series advantage. Following sloppy losses in Games 4 and 5, Jordan was determined not to let the Sonics' rally deepen any further. Game 6 was scheduled for Father's Day. Jordan took the extra motivation to the court and guided the Bulls to an 87–75 victory. It was their fourth championship in six years, and Jordan led the Bulls in scoring for 17 of 18 playoff games, earning his fourth Finals MVP honor. Sportswriters were beginning to refer to the Bulls as a dynasty.

On a Roll, Again

The Bulls continued to sail through their next regular season, finishing 69–13. Jordan averaged 29.6 points per game. He claimed his ninth scoring title but was denied another league MVP Award. That honor narrowly went to Utah Jazz forward Karl Malone.

Jordan appeared to hold a grudge, and he took it out on the Jazz when the teams met in the NBA Finals. The series featured Jordan at his competitive best. In Game 1, Jordan hit the game-winning shot at the buzzer, lifting the Bulls to an 84–82 victory. In Game 5, with the series tied at two games apiece, Jordan walked onto the court despite suffering from a stomach virus. Jordan had a high fever and was dehydrated at the opening tip-off. After crawling out of bed and needing help to get ready, Jordan found the energy to score 38 points. He also connected on the game-winning three-pointer with 25 seconds remaining, snagging a 90–88 victory.

Mr. Triple-Double

It did not take long for Jordan to record his first career triple-double. It happened at Chicago Stadium during his rookie season on January 14, 1985. In that game, Jordan recorded 35 points, 14 rebounds, and 15 assists. During his dominating 1988–89 campaign, Jordan recorded 15 triple-doubles. Over one stretch, Jordan had 10 in 11 starts. Jordan became the first player in NBA All-Star Game history to record a triple-double. He had 14 points, 11 rebounds, and 11 assists. For his career, Jordan had 28 triple-doubles during the regular season.

His energy zapped for Game 6, Jordan effectively played a decoy role. By drawing the attention of the defenders, Jordan's teammates opened up. At first they sputtered. The Bulls trailed through much of the opening three quarters. But in the final 15 minutes, they rallied. On a key play late in the fourth quarter, Jordan acted as if he would get the last shot. However, the play was designed to go away from Jordan. With defenders focusing on Jordan, open teammate Steve Kerr connected on the game-

Jordan shoots over Utah Jazz point guard John Stockton during the 1997 NBA Finals.

winning jump shot. Jordan and the Bulls had taken their fifth championship.

Jordan averaged 32.3 points per game in the Finals, despite his illness. He was named Finals MVP for the fifth time in five appearances. Jordan entered the off-season with another source of motivation: The Bulls were in position to repeat their "three-peat."

Double Three-Peat

As media and fan speculation again started swirling over his future, Jordan continued to turn in consistent performances during the 1997–98 season. On December 30, Jordan scored in double digits for the 788th consecutive game, breaking the record previously held by center Kareem Abdul-Jabbar. When the regular season ended, the streak increased to 840

Media Superstar

Jordan is perhaps the most successful product spokesperson of all time. Through the decades, he has been connected to such major brands as Nike, McDonald's, Gatorade, Hanes, Wheaties, and Ball Park Franks. Nike's Air Jordan campaign grew so popular over the years that the shoe company created a new division: the Jordan Brand. The brand is estimated to generate nearly $1 billion in sales annually for Nike. As of 2013, years after retiring, Jordan was still paid about $40 million per year for his endorsement work.

Defense Leads to Heroics

Jordan's defensive skills helped the Bulls secure the 1998 title. But as a freshman at UNC, Jordan struggled on defense. Dedication to improving his defense, year after year, made Jordan one of the top NBA defenders of all time.

games. The Bulls completed the season at 62–20 and entered the postseason as one of the favorites to capture the title. Many thought it would be Jordan's final postseason quest.

Jordan again cleaned up on MVP honors. He was named the NBA's top player during the regular season, the Finals, and the All-Star Game. He became the first player to achieve the triple honors twice during his career. With 29,277 points, Jordan moved into third place on the NBA's all-time scoring list. His scoring average of 28.7 points per game clinched his tenth—and final—individual scoring title.

In the Eastern Conference finals, the Bulls survived an intense seven-game series against the Indiana Pacers to make the Finals. The Finals would be a rematch from the previous spring, with the Bulls and Utah Jazz vying for the top spot. Through the opening five games, the teams exchanged momentum.

The Bulls entered Game 6 with a 3–2 series advantage. With 41.9 seconds remaining, Jordan and the Bulls trailed 86–83. Coach Phil Jackson called a time-out for the Bulls. He called Jordan's number. Jordan received the inbounds pass and drove hard to the rim, his tongue out, and scored over swarming defenders. The Bulls now trailed by one point as Malone took a pass and was doubled by Rodman and Jordan, who stripped the ball away.

In possession of the ball with time winding down, Jordan paused to examine the Jazz defense. He eyed defender Bryon Russell. Jordan cut right. Ten seconds remained. Jordan executed a crossover dribble and cut left for the series-clinching shot. Some say Jordan

Jordan Ranks among the Best

Entering the 2013–14 season, only four NBA franchises—Boston Celtics, Los Angeles Lakers, San Antonio Spurs, and Chicago Bulls—had captured more than three NBA championships. With six, the Jordan-led Bulls ranked third, behind the Celtics and Lakers. Jordan's six Finals MVP awards ranked first. Three other players—Shaquille O'Neal, Magic Johnson, and Tim Duncan— earned the honor three times each.

Jordan racked up many awards during his 13 seasons with the Bulls. He was a five-time league MVP, 10-time scoring champion, and three-time leader in steals and minutes played. Eleven times, Jordan was named All-NBA. Nine times, he appeared on the All-Defensive First Team.

pushed off on Russell, but a foul was not called. The high-arching jumper finally finished its journey through the net with 5.2 seconds to go. Jordan kept his shooting hand raised for several seconds in a scene that would go down in NBA history.

He finished with 45 points, and the Bulls won 87–86, duplicating their "three-peat" championship run. With growing speculation that Jordan would retire after the Finals, Game 6 had the highest television ratings of an NBA game in league history.

Jordan was awarded the 1998 NBA Finals MVP Award.

CHAPTER 9

Jordan joined the Washington Wizards as part owner and president of basketball operations in 2000.

Coming Back
One Last Time

It was time to go. A combination of issues led Jordan to retire from basketball for a second time in 1999. The Chicago Bulls' three-time championship core was coming apart. Coach Phil Jackson had decided to retire, and the contract for forward Dennis Rodman was expiring. Also, forward Scottie Pippen, Jordan's sidekick for all six championships, publically demanded to be traded. On top of all the Bulls' roster turmoil, there was threat of an NBA labor dispute between players and ownership groups. A lockout delayed the start of the season. Each day the lockout continued, the chances for Jordan returning dwindled.

On January 6, 1999, the labor dispute was finally settled, but Jordan had already made his decision. A week later, he called a press conference to announce he was retiring from the game. He said he was "99.9 percent" confident he played his last game.[1]

Over the next year, Jordan maintained a relatively low profile. He kept busy golfing, traveling, taking care of business ventures, and spending time with his family. About a year into his retirement, Jordan re-emerged as part owner and president of basketball operations for the Washington Wizards.

With the Wizards

A little more than a year later, in spring 2001, Jordan was in the midst of a grueling workout schedule. He was conditioning and weight training daily. He was playing basketball with friends and former teammates. When rumors started circulating Jordan would return to play for the Wizards, he initially laughed off the comments. Jordan insisted he just wanted to get back into shape and shed a few pounds he had put on while sitting in the front office.

Few were fooled. During the summer months, he was still training as he had a decade earlier. Since the NBA prohibits a player from owning share of a franchise, Jordan put credibility to the rumors he would return when he announced the sale of his minority share of the Wizards. On September 25, 2001, the 38-year-old Jordan officially announced he would play the 2001–02 season with the Wizards. Jordan was ready to come out of retirement—again.

Many fans, even some of his most loyal, were critical of the move. They feared he would tarnish his image as the world's best player. Jordan shrugged off the critics. He wanted to play again. He deeply missed the competitive nature of the game.

From the start, something seemed to be missing from Jordan's game. During the first few weeks of the season, Jordan was not playing like the old Jordan. The Wizards were not the strongest team, and they won only two of their opening 11 games. It soon became apparent that Jordan was suffering from knee problems. Rarely did Jordan drive to the basket, and he was not hitting his fadeaway jumpers like he had when he came back from his first retirement. Both Jordan and the Wizards overcame their slow starts. A few months of game conditioning appeared to be all Jordan needed.

During his first game back at Chicago's United Center on January 19, 2002, Jordan received a three-minute standing ovation. He later admitted to having a tough time playing against the Bulls at his previous home court. Jordan

Comparing Bryant to Jordan

Phil Jackson coached the Chicago Bulls and Los Angeles Lakers to 11 NBA championships. In his book *Eleven Rings: The Soul of Success*, Jackson compared two of the greatest NBA players: Jordan and Kobe Bryant. Jackson wrote: "Jordan was also more naturally inclined to let the game come to him and not overplay his hand, whereas Kobe tends to force the action. When his shot is off, Kobe will pound away relentlessly until his luck turns. Michael, on the other hand, would shift his attention to defense or passing or setting screens to help the team win the game."[2]

Although he was the oldest player on the team, Jordan often led the Wizards in scoring in 2001–02.

committed a career-high nine turnovers and scored just 16 points on 7-of-21 shooting.

Toward the end of February, Jordan underwent knee surgery and had to sit out for one month. Although he returned for seven games in March and April, the Wizards had slumped during his absence, finishing 37–45. They missed the playoffs. Despite his injury, Jordan paced the Wizards in scoring with 22.9 points per game for the season. He also led the team with 5.2 assists and 1.4 steals.

Jordan worked hard over the summer to return to his pre-knee injury game. "My love for the game of basketball continues to drive my decision [to play]," Jordan said. "I am feeling very strong and feel that the steps I took in the off-season have allowed me to return to the game in great condition."[3]

Jordan's Final Season

Jordan had a tough start to the 2002–03 season. In the opener against the Toronto Raptors, Jordan came off the bench and could not find his rhythm, going 4-for-14 from the field and 0-for-2 from the free-throw line. The Wizards lost 74–68, and sports networks replayed over and over a missed dunk he had during the game. Sports talk shows started discussing at length about how age and injuries cost Jordan some of the athleticism that helped him dominate for a generation.

Jordan was unfazed. He contributed 21 points the next game in a win over the Boston Celtics. Over the season's opening month, Jordan was still coming in off the bench, and he had not produced a 30-point performance. The media focused more on when Jordan would finally walk away than on his on-court performances. To end increasing speculation, Jordan called a press conference on Thanksgiving Day. He announced he would retire at season's end. "I just want to fulfill my year and enjoy it," Jordan said.[4] When Jordan was asked if there was any chance he'd return a fourth time, he responded, "Zero."[5]

Great Player

Although Jordan's tenure with the Washington Wizards was not the best of his career, he still demonstrated he was one of the greats. A few months into the 2001–02 season, Jordan showed flashes of youth, leading the Wizards to eight consecutive victories. In back-to-back performances, Jordan scored 96 points combined.

On January 4, 2002, Jordan scored 25 first-half points against his former team, the Bulls. During that barrage, Jordan collected his 30,000th career point. He was just the fourth player to reach that milestone, joining Wilt Chamberlain, Kareem Abdul-Jabbar, and Karl Malone. But in typical Jordan fashion, it was his defense that turned back a Bulls rally. As Bulls guard Ron Mercer drove to the basket, Jordan moved in position to apparently attempt a block. Jordan jumped and reached up. But he did not reject the layup attempt. He caught it. After the game, Jordan joked: "I was ticked. I can jump pretty high when I'm [ticked]."[6]

With that confirmation, Jordan's season turned into a series of tributes for the retiring superstar. Among his many moments, Jordan received a four-minute standing ovation at the Bulls' United Center. The Miami Heat also retired No. 23 even though Jordan had no ties to the franchise. Jordan was not voted a starter for the 2003 All-Star Game, but he was later inserted into the starting lineup thanks to Vince Carter. The Toronto Raptors' rising star took a seat for the aging superstar.

On February 21, 2003, Jordan became the first 40-year-old to score 40 points in a game when he had 43 against the New Jersey Nets. During his 15th and final season, Jordan was the lone Wizards player to appear in all 82 games. He averaged 20.0 points, 6.1 rebounds, 3.8 assists, and 1.5 steals. Over his final two seasons, Jordan did not lead the Wizards to the playoffs, but he did create a media frenzy around the franchise. All of Jordan's home games at the Wizards' MCI Center were sold out.

Last Game

Jordan suited up for his final NBA game on April 16, 2003, held in Philadelphia. Jordan struggled with his shot for most of the night. With just 13 points and the Wizards losing, 75–56, Jordan walked toward the bench with 4 minutes 13 seconds left in the third

More Time for Golf

When Jordan retired from playing for the third and final time in 2003, he had more free time to play golf. Golf had grown into one of Jordan's favorite pastimes. Jordan often recalled one of his early experiences learning the game. In 1983, he and fellow UNC student-athlete Davis Love III were on a course. Jordan did not yet have his own set of clubs. So he borrowed Love's favorite driver and addressed the ball. He swung hard and broke the future Professional Golf Association Tour champion's favorite driver.

quarter. There he remained, despite the crowd chanting, "We want Mike."[7] Jordan remained on the bench until coach Doug Collins encouraged him to re-enter one last time. Subbing for Larry Hughes with 2 minutes 34 second to go in the fourth quarter, players from both teams used the time to pay homage to Jordan.

Philadelphia 76ers guard Eric Snow went out of his way to foul Jordan and get him to the free-throw line. He hit both free-throw attempts with 1 minute 45 seconds to go. One second after the inbounds pass, another foul was called, and it wrapped Jordan's career. The players stopped the game so Jordan could walk back to the bench. The opposing crowd of 21,257, his rivals, and teammates gave Jordan a three-minute standing ovation to thank the player who had given them so much.

Jordan waves to the crowd as he walks off the court during his final game in the NBA.

Retirement has allowed Jordan more time for another of his athletic passions: playing golf.

Post-NBA Life

When Jordan announced his third retirement from the NBA, few fans or members of the media were shocked. It seemed like the right time for him to exit.

Jordan had plans of sliding right back into his role leading the Washington Wizards' front office. But Wizards owner Abe Pollin had other plans. Pollin was not impressed with Jordan's moves as a rookie president. Jordan's first major move had probably been his worst. He drafted 6-foot-11 Kwame Brown first overall in the 2001 NBA Draft. In doing so, Jordan passed on future stars such as Pau Gasol and Joe Johnson. As Brown failed to live up to his potential, Pollin lost confidence in Jordan's stewardship. Following a short meeting with Pollin on May 7, 2003, Jordan, essentially, was fired.

Drafting Brown was not Jordan's only mismanagement of players, Pollin believed. Jordan also played a role in trading Richard "Rip" Hamilton for an aging Jerry Stackhouse. Hamilton went on to lead the Detroit Pistons to the 2004 NBA championship. Propelled by Hamilton, the Pistons also appeared in six consecutive Eastern Conference championships. With Stackhouse, who was well past his prime, the Wizards went nowhere. After receiving Pollin's news, Jordan later said he felt betrayed. He said he never would have returned to play with the Wizards if he would have known his front-office fate.

Jordan stayed away from the NBA for the next couple of years. He remained active by playing golf and overseeing new business ventures, such as Michael Jordan Motorsports, a motorcycle racing company.

Hall of Fame Induction

Jordan was inducted into the Basketball Hall of Fame on September 11, 2009. The shrine in Springfield, Massachusetts, unveiled an exhibit dedicated to Jordan's milestones. It has items from his professional and college career. Jordan selected David Thompson to present him during induction ceremonies. Thompson, a former NBA star who played at North Carolina State, was Jordan's athletic hero when he was growing up. Thompson was inducted into the Hall of Fame in 1996.

During his induction speech, Jordan explained that he never forgot how some people, at difference stages in his life, doubted his skill set. That was what motivated him to succeed.

Showing up to show their support were former UNC coach Dean Smith and several former teammates, including Scottie Pippen, Steve Kerr, Ron Harper, Toni Kukoc, and Dennis Rodman.

Jordan gives his address during his Hall of Fame induction ceremony on September 11, 2009.

Team Owner

On June 15, 2006, Jordan made his way back into the NBA by purchasing a minority stake in the Charlotte Bobcats. Jordan also was named managing member of basketball operations and awarded full control of the team's basketball operations. Jordan wanted more. On February 27, 2010, Jordan reached a deal with owner Robert Johnson to purchase the majority share of the franchise. On March 17, the NBA Board of Governors approved the deal unanimously. Jordan became the first former NBA player to become majority owner of a franchise.

The Bobcats were hardly a model team under Jordan, though. They posted a 7–59 record during the lockout-shortened 2011–12 season. The team's .106 winning percentage was the worst in league history.

28 Game-Winning Shots

Over his 15-year profess-ional career, Jordan connected on 28 game-winning shots. Twenty-seven developed during the final 10 seconds and nine were buzzer-beaters. Jordan's first game-win-ner came a few weeks into his rookie season. On November 11, 1984, Jor-dan hit a 12-footer with four seconds remaining. The basket handed the Bulls a 118–116 victory over the Indiana Pac-ers. But when discussing game-winning shots, UNC fans will never forget his 16-footer with 15 seconds left in the 1982 NCAA championship triumph over Georgetown.

Jordan, to say the least, was frustrated. The building of the franchise continued, and so did Jordan's competitive nature. Following a Bobcats practice in February 2013, Jordan showed up ready for his next one-on-one challenge. Rookie Michael Kidd-Gilchrist took the bait. Now a business executive, Jordan was 49 years old. A prized first-round draft pick, Kidd-Gilchrist was 19. "I lost," Kidd-Gilchrist said. "It was hard on me. He's the greatest man that ever played the game."[1]

Jordan's Legacy

What is the legacy of the man who many people argue is the greatest basketball player of all time? Jordan was an all-around player who excelled at driving the lane, sneaking past opponents, shooting from outside, and pushing hard on defense. He had the leadership

Second Marriage

On April 27, 2013, 50-year-old Jordan married Yvette Prieto before more than 500 guests at a Palm Beach, Florida, church. Under a massive tent, the newlyweds entertained more than 1,500 guests at the reception. It was Jordan's second marriage.

to run an offense and the toughness to go up and grab a rebound. His charisma helped propel him to celebrity status in his early days of the NBA. Young athletes across the country wanted to be like Jordan with his effortless fadeaways and airtime.

He finished his 15-year career third in all-time scoring with 32,292 regular-season points. He also collected 5,987 postseason points. In 1999, ESPN named Jordan the greatest North American athlete of the twentieth century. He beat out athletic icons like Muhammad Ali and Babe Ruth. Jordan often credited his success to hard work and attention to detail in practice. He vowed never to allow an opponent to outwork him. It's safe to say, he achieved that goal.

Jordan's powerful and graceful dunks are part of his legacy.

TIMELINE

1963

Michael Jeffrey Jordan is born in Brooklyn, New York, on February 17.

1978

As a sophomore, Jordan fails to make the boys' varsity basketball roster for Laney High School.

1981

As a freshman, Jordan is in the starting lineup of the UNC basketball team.

1985

Nike unveils the Air Jordan shoe line.

1988

Jordan is named the NBA's MVP for the first time and the league's Defensive Player of the Year.

1991

Jordan and the Bulls win their first NBA championship.

1982

Jordan is named the ACC Freshman of the Year and hits the game-winning jump shot against Georgetown in the NCAA championship game.

1984

The Chicago Bulls select Jordan with the third overall pick in the NBA Draft.

1985

Jordan is named the NBA's Rookie of the Year after averaging 28.2 points per game.

1992

Jordan leads the Bulls to their second NBA championship.

1992

Jordan earns his second Olympic gold medal as a member of the Dream Team.

1993

Jordan leads the Bulls to their third-straight NBA championship.

TIMELINE

1993

Jordan retires from basketball for the first time.

1994

Jordan signs a minor-league contract with the Chicago White Sox.

1995

Jordan returns to the NBA with the Chicago Bulls.

1999

Jordan retires from the NBA for the second time.

2000

Jordan is named president of basketball operations for the Washington Wizards.

2001

Jordan returns to the NBA as a player for the Wizards.

1996

Jordan earns his fourth NBA championship with the Bulls.

1997

Jordan leads the Bulls to a fifth NBA championship.

1998

Jordan captures his sixth and final NBA Finals championship and his sixth Finals MVP Award.

2003

After two seasons with the Wizards, Jordan retires from the NBA for his third and final time.

2006

Jordan becomes part owner of the Charlotte Bobcats.

2009

Jordan is inducted into the Basketball Hall of Fame.

ESSENTIAL FACTS

DATE OF BIRTH
February 17, 1963

PLACE OF BIRTH
Brooklyn, New York

PARENTS
James Sr. and Deloris Jordan

EDUCATION
Emsley A. Laney High School (1977–81)

University of North Carolina at Chapel Hill (1981–84)

MARRIAGES
Juanita Vanoy, September 2, 1989 (divorced, December 29, 2006)

Yvette Prieto, April 27, 2013

CHILDREN
Jeffrey, Marcus, and Jasmine

CAREER HIGHLIGHTS

During his 15-year NBA career, Michael Jordan earned six championships, five MVP Awards, 14 All-Star Game appearances, and three All-Star Game MVP honors. Entering 2013–14, Jordan still held per-game scoring records for the regular season (30.12) and postseason (33.45).

SOCIAL CONTRIBUTIONS

Jordan has been linked to several charities and foundations, including Boys & Girls Clubs of America, CharitaBulls, Livestrong, Make-A-Wish Foundation, Nevada Cancer Institute, and the Special Olympics. Jordan also founded a Chicago-area YMCA in honor of his late father, James Sr.

CONFLICTS

During the peak of his NBA career, Jordan struggled with an apparent gambling addiction. Reports surfaced that he lost hundreds of thousands of dollars betting on golf. He also gambled in casinos and was in an Atlantic City casino the night before a 1993 playoff game.

QUOTE

"I've appreciated so much in my life from my family, from my kids, everything, but this is my most proud day I've ever had."—*Michael Jordan, after leading the Bulls to the 1991 NBA championship*

GLOSSARY

amateur
An athlete who is not paid to compete.

assist
A pass to a teammate that directly leads to a basket.

correspondence course
A class in which students receive lessons and assignments through the mail and return completed assignments to receive a grade.

draft
A system in sports in which each team in a league selects an incoming player. The order of picks is generally determined by the regular-season record, with the worst teams picking first.

dynasty
A team that wins several championships over a short period of time.

exhibition
A game that holds no competitive value, such as season rankings, for a player or team.

fadeaway
A type of shot in which the player shoots while jumping backward, away from the hoop.

foul
An infraction called for illegal personal contact or unsportsmanlike conduct.

free throw
A shot in basketball that a player takes after being fouled.

induct
  To admit as a member.

jumper
  A type of shot in which a player releases the ball in midair.
  These are commonly known as jump shots.

layup
  In basketball, a one-handed shot taken close to the hoop,
  typically using the backboard.

momentum
  Continued good play.

playoff
  A series of games played after the regular season by the best
  teams in a league in order to determine a champion.

rebound
  Gaining possession of the basketball after a failed shot.

rookie
  A first-year player in the NBA.

tempo
  The pace of motion or activity.

triple-double
  The accumulation of at least 10 accomplishments in three
  areas—such as points, rebounds, assists, steals, or blocks—
  in one game.

ADDITIONAL RESOURCES

SELECTED BIBLIOGRAPHY

Chansky, Art. *Blue Blood: Duke-Carolina, Inside the Most Storied Rivalry in College Hoops.* New York: T. Dunne Books, 2006. Print.

Lowe, Janet. *Michael Jordan Speaks: Lessons from the World's Greatest Champion.* New York: Wiley, 1999. Print.

Smith, Dean, and Gerald D. Bell with John Kilgo. *The Carolina Way: Leadership Lessons from a Life in Coaching.* New York: Penguin, 2004. Print.

FURTHER READINGS

Christopher, Matt. *Michael Jordan.* New York: Little, Brown, 2006. Print.

Jordan, Michael. *Driven from Within.* New York: Atria Books, 2005. Print.

Leahy, Michael. *When Nothing Else Matters: Michael Jordan's Last Comeback.* New York: Simon & Schuster, 2004. Print.

McCallum, Jack. *Dream Team: How Michael, Magic, Larry, Charles and the Greatest Team of All Time Conquered the World and Changed the Game of Basketball Forever.* New York: Ballantine Books, 2012. Print.

LEGENDARY ATHLETES

WEB LINKS

To learn more about Michael Jordan, visit ABDO Publishing Company online at **www.abdopublishing.com**. Web sites about Michael Jordan are featured on our Book Links page. These links are routinely monitored and updated to provide the most current information available.

PLACES TO VISIT

The Carolina Basketball Museum
450 Skipper Bowles Drive, Chapel Hill, NC, 27514
919-843-2000
www.goheels.com/fls/3350/museum/index.html?SITE=UNC
The museum celebrates the richness of UNC basketball, which Jordan contributed to for three years. Interactive presentations and player exhibits provide insight and history of the program.

Naismith Memorial Basketball Hall of Fame
1000 Hall of Fame Avenue, Springfield, MA, 01105
413-781-6500
www.hoophall.com
The basketball shrine details basketball's history and key events. The 40,000-square-foot space hosts numerous exhibits detailing the sport's inductees, including Jordan.

United Center
1901 West Madison Street, Chicago, IL, 60612
312-455-4500
www.unitedcenter.com
Home to the Chicago Bulls, the arena hosts a bronze action statue of Jordan, titled *The Spirit*, located near the main entrance.

SOURCE NOTES

CHAPTER 1. Dream Team Star

1. "NBA's Greatest Moments: The Original Dream Team." *NBA Encyclopedia Playoff Edition*. NBA Media Ventures, n.d. Web. 13 Aug. 2013.

2. Jack McCallum. *SI.com*. Time Inc., 25 July 2012. Web. 13 Aug. 2013.

CHAPTER 2. Growing Up

1. Matt Christopher. *Michael Jordan*. New York: Little, Brown, 2006. Print. 13.

2. Jeff Eisenberg. "Photos of Michael Jordan's Letter of Intent, Recruiting Letters." *Yahoo Sports!* Yahoo! Inc., 9 Feb. 2012. Web. 13 Aug. 2013.

3. Ibid.

CHAPTER 3. UNC

1. Dan McGrath. "Dean Smith on Jordan: 'He'd Listen Closely to What the Coaches Said and Then Go Do It.'" *Chicago Tribune*. Chicago Tribune Company, 10 Sept. 2009. Web. 13 Aug. 2013.

2. Jeff Eisenberg. "Photos of Michael Jordan's Letter of Intent, Recruiting Letters." *Yahoo Sports!* Yahoo! Inc., 9 Feb. 2012. Web. 13 Aug. 2013.

3. Dan McGrath. "Dean Smith on Jordan: 'He'd Listen Closely to What the Coaches Said and Then Go Do It.'" *Chicago Tribune*. Chicago Tribune Company, 10 Sept. 2009. Web. 13 Aug. 2013.

CHAPTER 4. Playing in the Pros

1. Terry Boers. "Here Comes Mr. Jordan." *NBA.com*. NBA Media Ventures, Jan. 1985. Web. 13 Aug. 2013.

2. Ibid.

3. Ibid.

4. Adam Fluck. "Rod Thorn Drafted Michael Jordan at No. 3 in 1984." *Bulls.com*. NBA Media Ventures, 3 Sept. 2009. Web. 13 Aug. 2013.

5. Ben Eagle. "50 Reasons Why We'll Never Forget Michael Jordan." *SI.com*. Time Inc., 15 Feb. 2013. Web. 13 Aug. 2013.

6. "NBA's Greatest Moments: God Disguised as Michael Jordan." *NBA Encyclopedia Playoff Edition*. NBA Media Ventures, n.d. Web. 13 Aug. 2013.

7. Ibid.

CHAPTER 5. Chasing the Championship

1. Jeff Merron. "Jordan: Between the Pages." *ESPN*. ESPN Internet Ventures, 9 Nov. 2004. Web. 13 Aug. 2013.

CHAPTER 6. Three Championships

1. Matt Christopher. *Michael Jordan*. New York: Little, Brown, 2006. Print. 76.

2. Ibid. 84.

3. Jack McCallum. *Dream Team: How Michael, Magic, Larry, Charles and the Greatest Team of All Time Conquered the World and Changed the Game of Basketball Forever*. New York: Ballantine Books, 2012. Print. 252.

4. Ibid. 252.

5. Ira Berkow. "Suddenly, Michael Doesn't Play Here Anymore." *New York Times*. New York Times Company, 7 Oct. 1993. Web. 13 Aug. 2013.

6. "The Michael Jordan Conspiracy Theory." *CBSSports.com*. CBS Interactive, 18 Feb. 2009. Web. 13 Aug. 2013.

CHAPTER 7. From Basketball to Baseball and Back

1. Matt Christopher. *Michael Jordan*. New York: Little, Brown, 2006. Print. 109.

2. "The Business of Michael Jordan: The Only Guy That Can Justify Selling a Jug of Barbecue Sauce For $10,000." *Trending Players*. Trending Players, n.d. Web. 13 Aug. 2013.

CHAPTER 8. Three More Rings

None.

CHAPTER 9. Coming Back One Last Time

1. "Michael Jordan Retirement Press Conference." *NBA.com*. NBA Media Ventures, 13 Jan. 2009. Web. 13 Aug. 2013.

2. Barry Petchesky. "Phil Jackson Finally Compares Michael Jordan and Kobe Bryant." *Deadspin*. Gawker Media, n.d. Web. 13 Aug. 2013.

3. Matt Christopher. *Michael Jordan*. New York: Little, Brown, 2006. Print. 135.

4. Ibid. 138.

5. Ibid. 138.

6. K.C. Johnson. "MJ's Gripping Finish." *Chicago Tribune*. Chicago Tribune Company, 5 Jan. 2002. Web. 13 Aug. 2013.

7. The Hip Hop Dynasty. "Michael Jordan's Last Game: A Day No One Will Ever Forget." Online video clip. *YouTube*. Google, 20 June 2009. Web. 13 Aug. 2013.

CHAPTER 10. Post-NBA Life

1. Matt Moore. "Michael Kidd-Gilchrist Says Michael Jordan Beat Him One-on-One." *CBSSports.com*. CBS Interactive, 16 Feb. 2013. Web. 13 Aug. 2013.

INDEX

ABOUT THE AUTHOR

Jeff Hawkins is a freelance writer who resides in Huntersville,
North Carolina. Hawkins is a former sportswriter who covered
the NFL's Carolina Panthers and NHL's Chicago Blackhawks.
Among his eight career writing awards, Hawkins was named
Associated Press Sports Editors' number one columnist for
Class C newspapers in 2005.

PHOTO CREDITS